ACROSS MY PATH

CONTENTS

CONTENTS

LIST OF ILLUSTRATIONS

MRS. JULIA WARD HOWE

IT sometimes happens that the reputation of a writer falls a slave to the one work that sprang in glowing spontaneity from the soul and struck upon the white heat of a Nation's crucial moment, sending an electric current thrilling through the heart of the world. So it happened to Julia Ward Howe, and to the great body of readers that name signifies the Battle Hymn of the Republic, though it was but the outglow of a momentary fire and her long, brave, laborious life was given by serious effort to the many great subjects which demanded the exercise of all the strength of her powerful mind.

"I should not think that you would like the Battle Hymn," she said when I spoke of it with praise.

"Why not? Do not you like 'Maryland, my Maryland'?"

1

"No; I do not. The poetry flats in places and the expression is not equal to the thought. And neither is the Battle Hymn an adequate expression of the feeling that gave it birth. I think written things never are. They fall short of the emotion which they strive to speak."

"I think the two poems must have been written under much the same kind of impulse," I said.

"Maybe they were. But I sometimes wonder if the Battle Hymn would have sprung into being had it not been for the impetus received from the casual suggestion of someone else."

"I fancied that it leaped out with no warning, as the flame towers up from the heart of a volcano."

"I felt so when it finally came to me. I was in Washington and, with some friends, among them my pastor, Dr. James Freeman Clarke, drove to a camp

2

near the city limits. As we returned some of our party sang a strain of the war-song, John Brown, and were cheered by soldiers along the way. Dr. Clarke turned to me with the query, 'Why do not you write some good words to that stirring air?' The thought had never occurred to me and it did not seem possible that I ever could write anything of that kind. I said, 'I wish I could,' with a feeling of dismissing the whole subject with the wish. I was tired that night and did not think about the Doctor's suggestion. I heard the tramp, tramp of soldiers' feet under my window at the Willard Hotel and soon fell asleep from fatigue. The next morning I awoke with the idea seething in my heart and bringing its expression with it. As the lines surged through me I knew that I must put them into form or they would drift away and never come again. I

3

got up and jotted them on paper and went back to bed and fell peacefully asleep."

"You must have had triumphant dreams in that sleep."

"No, I had no feeling but that of having relieved my heart of a fiery burden. It was later that the meaning of it began to dawn upon me, when I heard that Chaplain McCabe and his fellow-prisoners had sung it in Libby when the news of Gettysburg was brought to them, and that after his release, he had sung it in Washington before a large audience who had come to hear him tell the story of prison life, and the people sprang to their feet and wept and shouted and President Lincoln with tears flowing down his face called out, 'Sing it again!!' Then I realized that it is not the thing we write that carries weight, but that which writes itself through us."

4

"Great things would not select you to write themselves through if you had not been a student of lofty subjects and kept yourself in readiness to receive and give forth."

"But I had my frivolous time and enjoyed it as much as other girls enjoy theirs. I was so devoted to social pleasures that somebody said that if I were on a desert island with one old 'nigger' I would give a party. I shudder to think what would have been my mental state had not Doctor Howe rescued me as he rescued Laura Bridgman from blindness and deafness and put me back into the road on which I had been started by my early trainers when I used to make the maid tie me in a chair so that I could not leave my books and go out to play."

On being asked to give a motto for women Mrs. Howe replied "Up to Date." In her own career she illustrated the value of this motto, for she was never known to be out of touch with the interests of the moment and her help in every useful development was given with all the enthusiasm of her vigorous nature. She treasured the lessons of the past but never for a moment of her long life did she live in the past. Her pen and voice were always ready and efficient in promotion of the good cause and time did not leave her on the barren sands. The work she did in her last year was filled with the old strength applied to the new things of advancing thought.

MRS. JEFFERSON DAVIS

AT a reception in Richmond I stood beside Mrs. Davis as thousands of old soldiers passed by, stopping to give us the hand-clasp of affection and to look into our faces with eyes that held loving memories of past days and of those for whose sake we were dear to the veterans of the South. After they were gone she turned to me and said:

"Is not love the most wonderful thing in life? We should be the two proudest women on earth to have had the love of two such men as your husband and mine, who could inspire the hearts of so many, from the laborer with his rough toil-worn hand to the great professional man with soft white hand and strong brain, with such affection for us as is shown in the warm clasp and the loving eyes."

"And here we are, both forced to live apart from them, I in Washington because I must earn a living, and you still farther away."

"It seems strange to some that I live so far away from my old home and my southern friends, but it is not for lack of love. God ruled for the best in sending me to the North and Maggie to her western home. When she and her Confederate soldier husband went to Colorado they were not warmly received. The only thought in the community was that they had been of those who fought against the government. But she won them to friendliness and confidence and has built a monument to her father in the hearts of the people."

It has been so short a time since Mrs. Davis was taken from us we scarcely realize that her memory extended back to the days of men who passed from earth before the beginning of the war for which they had paved the way.

"About the time that Mr. Davis was elected to Congress," she said, "Mr. Calhoun came to Vicksburg and my husband was asked to welcome him in a speech. We became good friends and he deepened my always lively interest in politics. Our friendship involved me in difficulties, for I entered into a correspondence with him, and if you had ever tried to thread your way through the bewilderments of his complicated system of penmanship you would have some idea of my laborious efforts. After struggling in vain with a particularly involved epistle I returned it for explanation and he said, 'I know what I think on this subject but cannot decipher what I wrote.' I still clung to his friendship and was repaid for my constancy by the clearness of his expression when he was talking instead of writing. I quite agreed with Mr. Webster in the view that one of his greatest powers was in his conversation, but heaven help the unwary wanderer caught in the pitfalls of his writing."

"You escaped those dangers when you went to Washington where he could convey his thought to you without the medium of a pen."

"Think of the perils of traveling to the Capital in those days. We had no palace cars with velvet cushions and lofty porter to flourish a whisk broom in the air and demand a fee. We had to make a three-week journey in a carriage over rocks and mud-puddles and brambly ways. Falling down an embankment was a cheerful incident of our trip and our arrival at the National Hotel was surely an illustration of the 'survival of the fittest.' Mr. Davis took his seat in December,

10

1845, and—well, life was fairly interesting afterward, but that was a dear old home in Vicksburg."

"You have seen more of the world and its progress than you could have in quiet old Vicksburg."

"I saw the first telegram; one of my friends said she knew it was a trick, but put in two bits to get the news that it was a fine day. Somebody wrote me of a machine that sewed. I suppose some of the things that we regard as impossible will become as necessary to everyday life as the telegraph and sewing machine are now."

"It is interesting to watch things in the making."

"In New York, when we had gone north in the hope that the change might restore health to Mr. Davis, I saw the first cable message, 'Peace on earth, good will to men,' from the Queen of England, and again people thought it

11

was a joke played upon visionaries. At a picnic on the coast of Maine I found how widespread was my husband's fame as an orator. A servant upset a plate of cake over me and in apology confessed that he was only a student who had been told that Mr. Davis was to make a speech after tea and had asked the privilege of serving so that he might hear him. I forgave him and found a place for him where he could hear the speech without damage to the rest of us."

For a time the Davis family lived in the old Brockenbrough House near Richmond.

"It was a grand old place," Mrs. Davis said, "with beautiful terraced garden. Old Virginia gentlemen said, 'This house was perfect when lovely Mary Brockenbrough used to walk singing among her flowers.' We fell into the habit of referring everything to lovely Mary and consulting as to how she would like each change made. Not even here was peace; there was constant warfare between the 'hill cats,' on our knoll, and the 'butcher cats,' or lowland boys. The peaceful efforts of Mr. Davis were respectfully but firmly set aside. 'President,' said the leader of the "butcher cats," 'we like you and we don't want to hurt any of your boys, but we ain't never goin' to be friends with them "hill cats." ' "

The wit and intellect of Mrs. Davis made her a social leader in Washington for a decade or more before she was carried into the whirlpool of war. Her culture and ability brought into the Executive Mansion of the Confederacy a bright and congenial circle in which the weary President found diversion for an hour or two each evening before taking up the work which lasted far into the morning. He owed his life to

13

her devotion when he was a prisoner in
Fort Monroe. In after years she gave
him constant aid as an amanuensis and
brightened his life by her unfailing love.

HELENA MODJESKA

WE are indebted to the tyrants of the world for many gifted and charming people who have been forced upon our shores to seek the opportunities denied them in their own countries. To the Russian Government we owe the privilege of counting among our brilliant Shakspearian women the beautiful Polish actress, Helena Modjeska. She was called Helena because of her small Greek head which suggested the name famous in Grecian history and tradition, and Modjeska, a modified form of the name of the old man to whom her mother had married her in her very early youth. Through his appreciation of her talent she was greatly assisted in her stage career, which she had been permitted to enter after the death of her father, Michael Opido, and the loss

15

of the property on which the family income depended. Like most Polish women, Modjeska was enthusiastically patriotic, and so great was her popularity that the government feared her power, prohibiting her portrait to be shown in Warsaw, forbidding the students to attend her performances in a body, and shutting up the Polish theater in St. Petersburg just before her opening night.

"Such a little thing as I am," she said, drawing up her form to its not very great height, "for a big nation to be afraid of. Did you ever hear of such an absurdity?"

"The fatality of a charge of dynamite does not always depend upon the size of the package," I replied.

"The funniest thing that ever happened to me was in Ireland," she said, laughing. "I love the Irish, both for their characteristics and because they are, like my own people, oppressed; then again, they are fond of me. In Dublin I talked to them in the theater and they greeted me with applause and cheers. An English officer heard the noise and came in, thinking that I was saying something of a political nature. Fortunately I knew him and was not frightened when he came to me and told me that it was late and he had come to escort me home. I bade farewell to my friends and left the theater with my self-constituted protector, marveling by the way over the uneasiness of the head that wears the crown of despotism and wondering that anyone would ever consent to such discomfort."

Modjeska made her American debut as Adrienne Lecouvreur. From her success in that play and in Camille it was sometimes thought that she was essentially an emotional actress.

"I do not love those plays," she said.

17

"From the time I first saw Hamlet, Shakspeare has been my stage god."

"I have seen you play Rosalind and I should never know that you were the same person who breaks our hearts in those emotional plays. I think you like Rosalind."

"Yes, I do. I like to watch Orlando pretending to believe that he does not know who Ganymede is."

"Do you think he does know?"

"There is no doubt of it. Oliver had not succeeded in destroying Orlando's native wit, if he had refused to give him the training beseeming his station. He would know by intuition that the eyes that looked so earnestly into his were Rosalind's eyes. And if she were only the boy she pretended to be why should she have asked Orlando to fancy her to be Rosalind when she found that he was the love-lorn youth who had left his messages on every tree that offered

18

a page for the writing? If he did not know why did he accept the novel proposition? And then does not a lover know when he is in the presence of the beloved one?"

"Did not you once cheat the Count in that way?"

"Oh, the old peasant woman; wasn't she a joke?—clamoring for payment for her stolen pig, and that dear deluded man begging his host to pay the dreadful creature and get her away before Helena came, because she would keep them pig-buying all the afternoon, and never guessing that it was his worrisome Helena making all that bother. I arranged my disguise more carefully than Rosalind did hers, and then my Count had been bewildered by several years of trying to take care of me and his perceptions were blunted by hard usage."

Had Modjeska been less gifted as an

19

actress she could have devoted her life with equal success to any one of several other occupations. She wrote brilliant verse, painted pictures that would have made her famous but for her other great gift, amused herself by writing a charming fairy story and illuminating it by her own art, was an accomplished musician and composer, and wrote equally well in Polish and English. After the death of her guardian-husband she became Countess Pozenta Chlapowski, and she and the fascinating and scholarly Count made a beautiful home in California, which formed the nucleus of a Polish community on the founding and upbuilding of which the fortunes of the two were expended. There she died a few years ago and her own land, which could not give her a home, was permitted to open for her a grave.

CHARLOTTE CUSHMAN

I LOVE Boston and I know that you do."

"Yes, that was *my* home and there I made my first appearance on the stage. Shall I tell you the thing that pleased me most of all that ever happened to me? It is that the old house on Richmond Street where I was born is a school now and is named Cushman School. It is the first school in Boston to be named after a woman, and I think that is the greatest honor I could have. I was not in a reading part at first; I started out with the impression that I had a singing voice. People said that I had and when I tried it they listened as if they liked it. But it gave out down in New Orleans and I went to the manager of a theater and asked him for a place in his company. He had lost his Lady Macbeth and offered me the part if I could do it. The thought of playing Lady Macbeth filled me with such delight that I dared not tell him that I had no costumes for the character lest I should be prevented from taking it. I postponed the melancholy avowal until the day before the performance. He sent me to the leading lady of the French Theatre who was much amused by the idea of draping my lanky five and a half foot figure in robes designed for her stout four foot ten inch form, but she was good-natured and cut down and pieced out and otherwise maltreated her gowns until I was fitted out for Lady Macbeth, which unfortunate heroine I became when I was nineteen.''

''Was Lady Macbeth the character you liked best to play?''

''No; I preferred Romeo to all others. He has such a varied career and so many different emotions, and each

22

one is so tensely felt, that nearly all the facets of emotional life are presented. Then it gave me a chance to fight a real duel, which is always a triumph for a woman. On one occasion I experi enced an emotion not set down in the book. I was playing Romeo to Miss Anderton's Juliet when just as I was revealing the rapture of my love a man in the audience gave vent to a sneeze so loud and grotesque that I knew he had manufactured it for that occasion. I quit making love and led my lady off the stage with, I hope, a fair degree of the gallantry of the Montagues. I returned and announced that if some man did not put that person out I would have to do it. It was done and I got more cheers for that irregular interpolation than for any of the scenes written for the original Romeo. I escorted my Juliet back to the stage and the play went on.''

I noticed a black enameled ring that she always wore and she took it off and showed me the inscription on it, "Kind words. McVicker's Theatre, January 11, 1873."

"I caro moro for it than I could for a whole mine of jewels. Every word in it is a diamond of greater value than the Koh-i-noor and every line of tracery is a golden tendril of love. The dear people!—to think of the little I could do for them and to feel how I longed to be a real help and comfort to them! Their love was a lavish reward for the little word here and there which I could not have kept back if I had tried."

I knew that all the love that the mimic world could give would be slight recognition of what she had done for all who came near her. She was the good angel of the stage and no effort was too great for her if it brought comfort or help to someone else. While we were fellow guests in a delightful Richmond home I learned that her nobility of character, the womanly dignity of her manner and the love in her heart charmed all who knew her.

Macready said that when playing Macbeth to her Lady Macbeth he felt himself to be "less than of secondary importance—in fact, a mere thing of naught." The queen of the tragic stage, her own life was a tragedy, a long, agonizing battle with the disease that took her away all too soon from a world that can ill spare such as she. She died in her native city among the people who, as she said in her farewell to the stage, "from the beginning to the end of my career, from my first appearance on the stage to my last appearance, have been truly 'brothers, friends and countrymen.'" The plain granite shaft which marks her grave in Mount

Auburn bears no inscription except the name which stands for all that is brilliant in art, all that is noble and good in humanity, "Charlotte Cushman."

Yours sincerely
Adelaide Neilson

ADELAIDE NEILSON

ELIZABETH ANN BROWNE, mill-girl, nursery-maid, barmaid, seamstress, nameless member of a corps de ballet, doing Shakspeare in her leisure moments, and giving dramatic performances with her dolls for audience, could scarcely have looked forward to the time when she would be Adelaide Neilson, the one Juliet on the English-speaking stage, a radiant, Ariel-like spirit, the embodiment of spring, of dawn, of moonlight, of love and hope and dreams, the vision of the poet when he evolved that witching image of eternal youth. I marveled over her wondrous personation of that spirit of love and morning and sunshine, and once asked her:

"How did you learn to play Juliet so well?"

"Oh, one does not learn to play

27

Juliet. Either one is Juliet or is not;
that is all. The reason that Americans
have no Juliet is that they think she
must be learned and they do not create
an atmosphere in which she can be
born. The consequence is that an
actress spends years in trying to learn
Juliet and then when she essays the
part finds that she is long past the time
when there is a possibility of ever being
Juliet. If there was such a period in her
life it was away back when life was
young; when the sun had just risen on
the new day; when the rose was in the
bud and the dew lay sparkling on the
folded petal; when life was palpitant
with youth and the first dawnings of
love's vision; when all is emotion and
intuition and the cold and stony
prompter, Reason, has not appeared
with the whisper, 'But Juliet would not
have said it in that way; she would have
used a falling inflection here and an

emphasis there and an upward glance somewhere else.' When Reason takes hold of Juliet she dies more promptly than Romeo's dagger could have done away with her. There is a time in the life of every woman when she knows what Juliet would have done, and if she does not do it then—ah, it is too late!''

"I am glad that you selected the right moment and did not wait for time and reason.''

"Oh, but I did not select. No one ever selects in regard to Juliet. A man may select an appropriate opportunity for doing Shylock, or reason as to the proper way of reading Hamlet's soliloquy; a woman may study phrasing for the purpose of demonstrating the cruel ambition and subsequent remorse of Lady Macbeth, or compare different methods of representing the madness of Ophelia, but Juliet is an inspiration of the dawn, and is not due to any ability on the part of the one to whom the luminance comes.''

At the age of thirty-two the final curtain fell upon the drama of Adelaide Neilson's life and I have often thought of her words when I have seen elderly ladies frisking in springtime dalliance about their nurses and vowing undying affection to stout Romeos who are apparently on the verge of retirement for the blunder of obesity.

Neilson's voice, inherited from her Spanish actor-father, was filled with the music of song-birds and of soft winds at dawn, the joy of flowers opening in the sun and the sadness of long sea-waves breaking on the gray rocks on a day in dark November. That voice could touch the heart with joy and with sorrow, with radiant love or with fiery indignation. It was a melodious harp with strings that vibrated to every emotion.

Adelaide Neilson has passed from our sight but not from the stage world. She lingers there as the perennial Juliet. The traditions of that mimic realm are irradiated by her luminous eyes, her graceful form haunts the twilight of the Thespian gods as the Naiad Queen roams in the mystic shadows of an enchanted woodland. To those who knew her she is a radiant memory; to those who have come newly to the kingdom wherein she reigned she is a brilliant dream.

ADELAIDE RISTORI

I HAVE a cherished bit of lace, and sometimes take it out of its box and look at it, because it brings back to me one of the most glorious women I ever knew; glorious not only in her magnificent art, but in her lovely, gracious, deep-hearted womanhood. I like to see again in fancy her stately form, her wealth of shining, chestnut hair, the luminous deep lakes that Italians have for eyes. I love to watch once more the flashes of lightning glancing across them when the passion of her art thrilled her. It is a delight to live again in the magnetic personality that made Ristori the most fascinating figure on the stage of her era. She comes back to me sometimes when I look at little children, for she loved children with a great big affectionate heart.

"Though," she said laughing, "the

ADELAIDE RISTORI

little angels have at times almost wrecked my professional career, just as I used to do in the beginning of my stage life when the fate of some poor victim depended upon my histrionic integrity. Children do such unexpected things. I had one in Medea once who upset all my tragic effects. One of the children had a speaking part and as there was only one infant actor in our company we gave him the talk and borrowed a child from the neighborhood for the silent one. When the crisis arrived I turned my back to the audience and was supposed to be killing my offspring in approved style, when the little stranger, being seized with stage fright and possibly fearing for his life in my deadly hands, jumped up screaming and ran with all speed across the stage and took refuge in a wing. The audience had been much impressed by the tragic scene, but what human could

view calmly a dead child springing up
without warning and rushing across the
stage? A wave of laughter submerged
that scene. I could not complain, for
I had hopelessly ruined the first scene
in which I appeared, at the age of
three months, in a New-Year's gift bas-
ket, in which I had been introduced into
the family with the poultry and fruit
for the purpose of establishing peace
between my reckless parents and my
hard-hearted grandfather who had
never forgiven them for eloping and being married without his consent. Instead of diffusing peace over the situa-
tion, I immediately declared war by
shrieking my loudest and completely
drowning the voices of the more experi-
enced actors, while the audience went
into convulsions of laughter. It's a bad
thing artistically for an audience to
laugh when the play does not call for
mirthfulness. Sometimes it puts peo-

34

ple into a good humor and makes them more friendly to a play that needs charity. But to laugh in Medea—Oh, the pity of it!"

In the horror of the thought Ristori looked as tragic as if she were again the Colchian Princess putting her beloved children to death.

The sympathetic heart of the child of sunny Italy went out to all in trouble. One of her happiest triumphs was in saving the life of a poor soldier who was under sentence of death for placing his hand on the hilt of his sword when his superior officer had struck him unjustly. At the theater between the acts one evening at Madrid she laid aside her stage character and appeared in the Queen's box in a tragedy greater than any of the Shakspearean rôles that she loved to play. Throwing herself at the feet of the Queen she begged for the life of the unfortunate man. After a time so long that the audience became impatient she secured an order for commuting the sentence, which reached the prison just as the priests were administering to the condemned man the last service of the Church.

"But that only saved his life," she said. "He was sent to prison under a life sentence. Six years later when the Prince of the Asturias was born I visited the Queen again and implored her to pardon the man who had been so severely punished for so slight an infraction of military rules. She graciously granted my plea and the man became my devoted friend and whenever I played in Madrid would sit in the gallery applauding so wildly as to awaken the curiosity of his neighbors. 'She saved my life,' he would reply to inquiries as to his enthusiasm. A pleasing incident of his prison life was an apology and plea for pardon from the

36

officer responsible for the injustice. In an illness that threatened to be mortal he had repented of his cruelty and wished forgiveness."

Ristori was past the half century mark when she began the study of English and she spoke it with an accent that may have been a defect in Lady Macbeth, but it was delightful, and wholly unrepresentable, in the conversation of the brilliant Italian.

Born to the stage, Ristori was at fourteen taking leading parts and at eighteen she played Mary Stuart, though upon her first appearance as the unhappy Queen of Scots her manager told her that she had a marked tendency for comedy but "as for tragedy, it is not for you, and I advise you to abandon it entirely!" She may have reflected upon the lack of prophetic soul at times manifested by managers, years later when she was the queen of tragedy,

37

with the elder Dumas kissing the hem
of her mantle and cooking macaroni
for her, Legouvé worshiping before her
shrine, Jules Janin expressing his opin-
ion that "she lacks nothing but to be a
French woman," and the famous Clé-
singer announcing delightedly, "I will
break the statue of Tragedy I have
made, for Ristori has taught me that it
was but the statue of Melodrama!"

MARY ASHTON LIVERMORE

SAID one of her admirers, "The only fault that Mrs. Livermore has is that knowing her makes all other women seem insignificant." There was a magnitude in Mrs. Livermore's nature that caused her to be regarded as above the rest of humanity, yet not too far away for any wounded or wearied soul to lean upon her and find support. She was granite to uphold but tenderly human to sympathize and love.

She wore a gold ring which testified to her depth of feeling and the appreciation that it elicited from those whom she served. Some years after the close of the war between the States, upon the conclusion of a lecture delivered by Mrs. Livermore in a community to which she was a stranger, a woman came to her and asked if she remembered a

letter that she had written to the wife
and mother of a dying soldier, giving
his name. Mrs. Livermore had written
so many letters for soldiers who would
never again see their dear ones on earth
that she could not recall this one until
the woman showed her the old letter,
worn and patched, but still legible.
"I recall that letter," said Mrs. Livermore. "I hope that it brought at least
a little comfort to you." "It helped us
to live through that awful time. It
has helped others. We sent it to those
who had suffered like sorrow until it was
so worn that I had to sew the paper together. Then I quit sending it out, and
made copies for those who might be
aided by your loving thought and tender words. The poor young wife kept
up for a few years and then died of sorrow. On her deathbed she told me to
take her wedding ring which she should
wear until her death, and give it to you

as a token of remembrance of your
goodness to our soldiers. So, when I
found you were coming I made up my
mind that I would hear you and give
you the ring," handing her a circlet of
gold, which Mrs. Livermore accepted
tearfully and lovingly.

"You have had an eventful life," I
said to her. "Please tell me some of the
thrilling and soulful things you have
known."

"I think," she said, "the time of
greatest excitement I have ever known
was in the Wigwam in Chicago when
Abraham Lincoln was first nominated
for the presidency. To me the most remarkable feature of the occasion was
my being there, so close to the center of
action. There were women in the gal-
leries stretched away in so large a circle that they could not hear anything
that went on except the shouting when
it was all over. Greatly to my surprise

I was sent by my paper to report the Convention. It was the first time a woman had ever been appointed to report a meeting of that kind. So unheard of a thing could not pass unquestioned and the Marshal of the day came to me and told me that I must go into the gallery, as women were not allowed on the floor. My husband, who was reporting for his own paper, tried to explain my position but was not permitted to do so. The other reporters came to my defence and told me to sit still and recommended the Marshal to 'dry up,' as they expressed it. So I stayed in the heart of the battle and witnessed every scene and heard every word. The Wigwam was packed. An immense crowd was gathered around the building, and sentinels posted upon the roof to give the signal to the throngs below when the decisive moment should come. It came. It seemed to me that the mighty

42

shout arising from that great throng
went around the world and came back
with renewed strength and resonance.
Thus I saw Mr. Lincoln on his most
triumphant day, and yet not in triumph, for his face showed a sadness
such as I had never seen on any other,
and the pain and weariness of it impressed me more and more every time
I saw him afterward. I recall his saying, at a time when the darkness was
heaviest around him, 'Oh, if there is a
man out of hell that suffers more than
I do I pity him!' "

Mrs. Livermore was a leading worker
in the Sanitary Commission Fair to
which President Lincoln sent the original manuscript of the Emancipation
Proclamation, thereby winning the
prize offered by a gentleman of Chicago
for the largest single contribution, a
gold watch, which the President wore
with great satisfaction. He had prom-

ised Mrs. Livermore that he would be present at a fair to be given in May, 1865, but before the time arrived his premonition that he would not live long after the close of the war had been tragically realized.

In passing from earth Mary Ashton Livermore left a memory that is a rock of strength and a garden of blossom and fragrance to the many who knew her as a friend and the many more who from afar felt the influence of her good deeds and noble character.

Laura Keene

LAURA KEENE

A COMEDY character of the highest type, it was the unhappy fate of Laura Keene to have a part in the most terrible tragedy that has ever plunged our Nation into darkness. Though she lived nine years afterward and played with her old fire, she never recovered from the shock of that night. The blood that saturated her stage costume as she held the wounded head of President Lincoln was a crimson river that flowed through the rest of her life.

Stuart Robson said of her: "I consider Laura Keene to have been in many respects the most able woman connected with the stage of her time. Her best impersonation was perhaps Peg Woffington in 'Masks and Faces.'" To have learned the long list of plays in which she appeared would be no light task for anyone, and when we reflect upon her wide range of characters, from Shakespeare to the newest light comedies, and upon the fact that she was also one of the best theater managers of her day and a brilliant writer on art subjects, we can but wonder over the varied abilities which she displayed.

"Oh, but one must know how to manage many things if one is to put a play through successfully. Think of that night that we were to open in 'Much Ado about Nothing' and the men's clothes were not ready! If I had not been something of a manager what could I have done but collapse? I didn't, though; I just called all those people around and set them to work upon the costumes and then finished off with paint and put those men far enough apart not to rub each other off and then went away to don my Beatrice robe and nobody in that audience ever knew that those fancy clothes were not straight from the costumers, constructed after the most approved style."

"That was a triumph, certainly," I admitted. "And people say that you have the most beautiful theater in the world."

"I do try to make it a home. Why not? When we poor players have to spend all our waking hours in a theater we do not want it to be like a barn. We want graceful draperies and vines and flowers and soft lights and all those things that come sweetly to the mind at the thought of home. Does it occur to you sometimes that the inadequacy of some actors who really have talent is due to the rough and bare surroundings in which they spend their lives? They have the feeling of homelessness and so are never quite at home in their parts."

Laura Keene had the good fortune to live in a time when actors presented a play instead of a wardrobe. It mattered more that they should surround a character with a new fresh atmosphere than that they should surround themselves with gorgeous new suits of clothes fresh from the shop of the leading tailor. Players then were real live human beings with thought and feeling lurking somewhere in their intellectual and emotional systems.

"You really do feel what you speak and act," I once said after hearing her in an emotional part.

"Otherwise I could not speak and act," she replied. "Oh, I can be practical enough to wait in the wings until I am sure of my money, but before the footlights I forget all about Laura Keene with a whole world of sordid necessities in everyday life, and really fancy myself 'Beatrice' or 'Rosalind' or 'Peg' with a world of totally different interests."

48

Had Laura Keene been less versatile she might have fared better and, perhaps, lived a longer life. Leaving the stage for a time she gave herself up to the Fine Arts periodical which she founded and edited. It was intended for readers who were interested in the high phases of art, dramatic and otherwise, and only the art thinkers gave it support. It soon vanished, and with it much of Laura Keene's money. She had lived up and burned out her life in a shorter time than it takes most people to reach that end and she passed from earth when she should have been in the prime of her genius.

JEAN DAVENPORT LANDER

WHEN Mrs. Lander was playing an engagement in Richmond Mrs. Allan gave a tea, inviting her guests to meet the actress, who was a social favorite as well as a theatrical star. I chanced to be sitting by Mrs. Lander when tea was served on little tables placed before us to hold the delicious viands which our hostess had prepared for us.

"How very delightful this is," said Mrs. Lander. "It gives me a beautiful chance to talk to you, and we can say friendly and intimate things under the inspiration of the tea-cups. What pretty little biscuits! I have heard of Maryland biscuit; are these the same?"

"I have never eaten Maryland beaten biscuit but they originated in Virginia and our neighbor Maryland borrowed the recipe."

"Then I shall eat them with a clear Virginia conscience and a good appetite," replied Mrs. Lander with an air of entire satisfaction.

Opposite us was a window from which the swift-seeing eyes of the actress were reveling in one of the most beautiful views in Richmond.

"How exquisite!" she said softly. "And this is Poe's old home."

"It was for a little while," I replied, "when it was quite new and he was on the verge of life, with dreams and hopes and visions in his soul."

"There is sunshine and beauty enough in that view to permeate a man's whole life, wherever it may have been spent afterward. How could he ever have seen anything but light and joy in the world?"

"I think he had a world of his own," I said, "into which he turned his vision and found things that no one else

51

would have discovered in a whole universe.''

''And such weird, ghoulish objects he saw,'' mused Mrs. Lander, ''and sometimes such wondrously beautiful things, more beautiful than anyone else could have found. His pictures were so vivid; if they were views of frightful things they were so real that we were terrified by the strength of them; if they were visions of the golden side of life we were dazzled by their brilliance and beauty.''

A one-armed veteran at a table near came over to speak to us and as he went back to his place I saw Mrs. Lander's eyes follow him with a sad light in them and knew that she was thinking of her soldier-husband, General Frederick West Lander, who died in the second year of the war. After his death she and her mother had charge of a hospital at Port Royal. The loving remembrance which followed her through the rest of her life for the work that she did in caring for sick and wounded soldiers was dearer to her than all the fame she won in her art. In 1865 she returned to the stage in her own translation of "Mésalliance." She was the first to produce in the United States Browning's "Colombe," Reade's "Peg Woffington," Hawthorne's "Scarlet Letter." In the great characters of "Adrienne Lecouvreur," "Marie Stuart," "Medea" and "Queen Elizabeth" she rivaled Ristori. In her childhood Jean Davenport was called "the little Dramatic Prodigy" and it was said that she suggested to Dickens the character of the "Infant Phenomenon."

Though English by birth, leaving a successful European career when she first came to America in her girlhood, she became to all intents an American and when, after many brilliant years on the stage, she made her farewell appearance in the Boston Theater in the "Scarlet Letter," she found a home in Washington, where she spent the remainder of her life surrounded by many friends who remembered with admiration her strong and intellectual interpretation of "Rosalind" and her stately and classic presentation of "Lady Macbeth," and were won to a deep and personal love by the noble qualities of her character.

MADAME JANAUSCHEK

FANNIE JANAUSCHEK

THREE stars blazed with dazzling brilliance in the theatrical sky of the middle Nineteenth Century; Rachel, whose early death robbed the French stage of its greatest tragedienne while yet at the height of her career; Ristori, who belonged to the world and loved it and reveled in it through eighty-four sparkling years; and Janauschek, the most stately figure of all, whose life went out in the darkness of defeat and loss. One of her auditors well expressed the effect of her work by saying, "I shall always look back on some of the occasions on which I have seen her as among those which afforded me fullest gleams of the possible greatness of the stage." The Muse of Tragedy who had inspired the soul of Shakspeare to the highest expression of the grandest ideals of the stage had endowed her with equal power in the personation of those ideals.

Unlike most great actresses, Madame Janauschek had a husband whose first aim in life was to serve her interests and she was gifted with a heart to appreciate his devotion, notwithstanding the Herculean qualities of her mind, which made her the strongest actress of her time. When she was playing in Richmond she used to come from her room to mine in the Ballard and Exchange Hotel for friendly converse.

"Mr. Pillot's greatest dread is that he may be taken for 'Janauschek's husband,'" she said. "He says, 'I am more than that; Madame Janauschek is my wife.' Is not it delightful to have a husband who is so proud of me that he wants all the world to know that I am his? He will not even let me use my earnings for any of my own expenses. He gives me everything and puts my money carefully away for my use when I may need it. Better than all else, his devotion to me smooths all the roughness from my path and plucks the thorns from my roses."

"To have such love and so great fame seems almost too much happiness for one woman," I said.

"Ah, there are discordant notes in the chorus of fame," she replied, "but there is only harmony in the song of love."

It always surprised me that so loving a woman and one so devoted to children could be the born Medea or Lady Macbeth. I could never imagine her as killing her children or expressing her willingness to sacrifice her infant for the lure of ambition. I have a poem, copied in her own handwriting, "The Mother of an Angel," which she gave me just after the death of my little boy.

"Could there be anything more beautiful," she said, "than to be the mother of an angel? It must be the greatest of joys to feel that a little soul that belongs to you is in heaven sending down to you white roses of loving thoughts and coming nearer to you as he grows more and more into the higher phase of life; loving you more and more as he expands into the luminous life which is love."

She waved her hands in that graceful way with which she tried to express a thought that was too deep and high for words—even her words.

Janauschek was not one of those handsome stage women who win admiration by physical attractions. She had no charm of appearance to equal the Jewish beauty of Rachel or the exquisite Italian loveliness of Ristori. But in the presence of her wonderful expression, her graciousness and her irresistibly impelling voice one never thought of any lack of other attractions. On the stage she was the character that she enacted and in the mind of the audience was just what that figure must be, regardless of any traditions as to appearance.

The great Bohemian had brighter promise of a happy and successful career than any of her contemporaries on the stage, but the close of her days was the most tragic of all. One must weep over the early passing of Rachel from the scene of her triumphs, but she left the stage with its glamour yet veiling it in iridescent hues and the dew still sparkling on the roses that crowned her youthful head. Janauschek lingered till all the illusions were shattered and her triumphs belonged to the past. The lover-husband who had shielded her from the sordid cares of existence died while she was in her prime of work and success. Great genius is rarely allied with the faculty for the trivialities of financial management. At the last she had only her magnificent jewels to ward off the wolf from the door. She died in a sad isolation, unbroken even by members of her own profession, usually the surest to remember and the most generous in kind action. With her passing Lady Macbeth left the stage, probably forever.

FANNY KEMBLE

SHE was christened "Frances Anne"
but it is not likely that the name
was over thought of in connection
with her after it had been registered.
She was Fanny Kemble to all the world,
and the name signified the concentra-
tion of the genius of a line of histrionic
ancestry. I met her at the home of
Mrs. Elias Hook in Boston, where a
number of guests had met, among them
Dr. Oliver Wendell Holmes, Mrs. Julia
Ward Howe, Mrs. Kate Tannatt Woods
and Bishop Phillips Brooks.

"I like your southern accent," she
said.

"And I like your English accent."

"You could acquire my English accent if you tried, but I never could learn
your southern accent. I lived for over
a year in Georgia on a rice plantation,
and while I learned of the suffering be-

cause of slavery, I knew, too, that sufficient justice was not done to the kind master upon whom slavery had been thrust. Harriet Martineau and I used to have some bitter differences on that subject.''

"Do you know Harriet Beecher Stowe, 'the little woman who made the war,' as Mr. Lincoln said?"

"Ah, yes; the first time I ever met her was at a grand reception given me in Arlington Street. She came in from the train, dressed in a plain, coarse, black gown, but one seeing her sweet classic face, hair parted in the center and waving and ending in loose curls about her neck, forgot her gown.''

"I knew and heard Charlotte Cushman and she told me about you, but I never hoped to meet you. I wish I could have seen you play."

"You saw in Charlotte Cushman the greatest tragic actress of the world.

62

She made her debut here and is, I believe, the only Boston woman who has ever attained international success on the stage. When I first came to Boston in 1832 under the management of Mr. Thomas Barry I met your John Howard Payne. At that time he had just returned after a twenty years' absence and was given a benefit a few days before my appearance."

"Your art gives you an opportunity of meeting all the charming people as well as of having such beautiful experiences."

"When I told Mr. Washington Irving that I did not like the stage because it gave me no time for congenial and improving work he said that I was seeing the world and by and by I could retire and give myself to a happier career but, great as Mr. Irving was, he was not a prophet."

"Perhaps he was not so bad a sooth-sayer. In the time you have had for quiet life and work you have made more progress than you could but for your knowledge of life and people and the outside world.

"Quiet life does not come to any of us. We never had any real life. I think if we could trace our family back to the Garden of Eden we should find the original Kemble in a mocking-bird that spent his life imitating the sounds he heard and pretending to be any kind of bird that he was not. We have been somebody else so long that we never find ourselves."

"It is beautiful to be able to be any kind of bird at will. It expands the sympathetic nature and makes life varied and interesting."

"If one could feel, with my Aunt Sarah Siddons, that there is nothing worth living for but upturned faces in

the pit it would be the ideal life. She
was the goddess of my childhood. I
was not a good child. I intended to be
but native instinct and adverse fate
were against me. Once I had been unusually fractious and was turned over
to my Aunt Sarah for reproof. She
took me on her lap and talked to me
seriously, giving me wise advice, I suppose, but I did not hear a word she
said for looking at her exquisite face.
When she paused to note the effect of
her lecture I exclaimed in a rapture of
admiration, 'What lovely eyes you
have!' She gave me up in despair, put
me down on the floor and walked off
laughing. I was not a born actress; I
went on the stage because I had to do
something and there was nothing else
for me.''

''You had the talent, at least; I have
heard that you were the real Juliet herself when you were sixteen and six

weeks after you first thought of going on the stage.''

''That was because my beautiful father was my Romeo and my mother came out of her years of retirement just to be Nurse for me. Now, I was born for the life at Lenox. I could even practice art better on that natural stage than anywhere else. The old boatman who used to take me out on Laurel Lake to fish said that no one knew anything about me who had never heard me on the Lenox Mountains. The reason was that I lived in Lenox; in other places I only appeared. Lenox disappointed me only once; that was when I gave a reading for the benefit of the poor in the community and discovered too late that there were no poor and that the people were offended by my well-meant efforts to do good. After that I waited till I found the sore before applying the healing plaster of charity.''

With the proceeds from her readings the radiant Fanny purchased a cottage in Lenox and spent her latest years there in recording the events of her long and varied life and in her peaceful, studious seclusion succeeded in "finding herself," as she had wished.

ANNA CORA MOWATT

THE beautiful Anna Cora Mowatt, whom we knew as a retired actress in Richmond, had not that innate love of the stage which characterizes those who achieve such brilliant careers in the mimic world. Through the influence of a pastor of rigid views upon the subject she had been imbued with the impression that the theater was the center of all evil.

"The first time I ever felt even the slightest willingness to subject myself to contact with so wicked a thing was when Fanny Kemble was playing in a theater near our home. I wanted to see her more than I had ever wanted anything else, but dared not let my wish be known through fear of being laughed at for wanting to see something of which I had always before expressed so strong a disapproval. As I walked one

Anna Cora Mowatt Ritchie

day with my older sister, our father came to us and asked her if she would like to go to see Fanny Kemble. I wished that he would ask me, but he went on talking as if so wild an idea could not occur to him. After awhile he turned to me and said, 'I suppose you would not care to go.' I admitted that I should like to see the divine Fanny and so received my first invitation to the theater and yielded to the fascination of that most brilliant creature."

"Did you become an enthusiastic theater patron from that time?"

"No; I thought Fanny Kemble could glorify anything, but my sentiments in regard to the stage in general remained unmodified. When sorrow fell upon me and want came uncomfortably near I gave public readings, but when success brought me a flattering offer to go upon the stage I felt almost offended, though

I trust that I declined with a proper feeling of gratitude."

"But you wrote for the stage," I said.

"It was the success of my play 'Fashion' that first suggested my going into stage work. I wanted to view things from the sublime standpoint of the omniscient actor who knows so much better what the playwright means than he does himself, and smiles at the hallucination of the feeble-minded author that he knows the meaning of his own words. Three weeks after I had determined to take up the work I appeared in 'The Lady of Lyons' with but one rehearsal. When the play was over the audience all rose and showered a wealth of flowers over me."

"Such beautiful things happen to stage ladies, don't they?"

"Sometimes; and then again things are not so pleasant. I used to think

70

that the property man was the one infallible memory freak who could not possibly forget anything. This illusion remained with me until one evening when I was playing Juliet that Infallible One forgot the bottle containing the sleeping potion. Some kind of a bottle was necessary and the property man picked up the first at hand and shoved it over. At the words, 'Romeo! This do I drink to thee!' I placed the bottle to my lips and swallowed the draught. When the scene closed the prompter rushed up with the cry, 'Good gracious! You have been drinking from my bottle of ink!' I felt like the dying wit who, having been accidentally given ink instead of medicine, asked for a piece of blotting paper which he might swallow."

As a child, notwithstanding her aversion to the stage, Anna Cora was the playwright and star of the Mowatt family cast, though she said that her little sister Julia had the greatest talent in the household. Her play of "Gulzara" had no hero, the only male character in it being a boy of ten years, put in to be played by the little Julia. "But I do not want her to go on the stage," said the actress, whose brilliant success had never won her heart away from the home life that she loved and had relinquished when the companion of that life had lost fortune and wealth and was compelled to give the reins of business government into her unaccustomed hands. Well did she accomplish her task, retaining all the while the same loving heart and faithful devotion that had inspired her when at fifteen she had given her life to the chosen one.

ELLEN TREE

ELLEN TREE, known off the stage as Mrs. Charles Kean, was more continuously enveloped in stage atmosphere than anyone else I have ever known. Others forget at times that they are actresses, or remember it with a sensation of relief that they can now and then throw off the mimic part and be themselves by way of variety. She used to stab the butter with the knife in a manner which suggested that she was doing deadly things to some unfortunate stage villain. She would order a spool of thread in a voice that threw the clerk into a nervous chill from which he recovered with difficulty and the assistance of a physician. She impressed me with the idea that she slept on the verge of a volcano in eruption with thunderstorms sweeping over her and an earthquake shaking her couch.

73

I first saw Ellen Tree in Canada when General Pickett and I were exiles, known by an assumed name, "Edwards," his middle name. One evening when I was putting baby, who was unusually fretful, to sleep she came in with a "Banquo-is-buried-and-cannot-come-out - of - his - grave" manner and said, "The child,—is't ill, or doth it need the rod withal?" He seemed to need nothing but her startling presence, for he immediately quit crying and fixed his eyes upon her face until he was hypnotized to sleep. She invited the General and me to the theater that evening to see her and Mr. Kean in "Hamlet." Meeting her after I had returned to my own country and name she said:

"You look so much like a Mrs. Edwards whom I met in Canada. When I was there again I tried to find her and the dear little baby, George, who had such peachy cheeks and glorious eyes,

74

but they had gone and I could find no trace of them."

"I am Mrs. Edwards," I replied, and explained the name by which she had known me and introduced her again to the little boy whom she remembered as a baby, and who still had the "peachy cheeks and glorious eyes." She was very glad to see us again and have a pleasant talk of the old Canadian days.

"How you made me cry my eyes out and then in the farce Toodles made me laugh until the tears came again," I said.

"I am glad that you laughed afterward," replied Ellen, "for I do not like to send my audience home crying; it seems too ill a reward for the goodness of people in filling theaters for me and it is unkind to make folks unhappy."

"I thought you were unhappy, too. I am older now and have learned that people, both on and off the stage, learn to simulate unhappiness at will."

75

"But I was unhappy, I suppose," returned Ellen. "I recall one play in which it was my sorrowful fate to see my husband die in the last scene. He was not only my play husband but my own Charles off the stage. It would seem that I might have been accustomed to the bereavement by that time, having suffered it often before, but I threw myself upon the body in a burst of uncontrollable grief, wildly imploring him to tell me that he was not dead. He gave the desired information in terms so emphatic and so nearly verging upon profanity that I felt instantly assured that he was not anywhere near dissolution. The audience could not hear what he said, and took my passionate grief for a part of the play, so I let myself be carried off the stage amid enthusiastic applause. When the only mourner over Mr. Kean's lifeless body was his faithful dog the illusion

76

was lost and the audience went off into fits of laughter that quite ruined the tragedy. Mr. Kean's dog loved him with a devotion of which not many human hearts are capable. Watching from the wings, the faithful animal saw his master fall under the attack of the stage villain whose histrionic duty was to kill the star with a dagger thrust. Rushing out the dog bestrode the dead man and snapped viciously at the murderer whose next business was to carry off the inanimate body. As the dog could not be coaxed to leave his dead master and the actor dared not approach the ferocious guardian, the curtain hastily fell amid the laughter and uproarious plaudits of the spectators. That was the dog's first and last appearance upon any stage, but if a human actor had made so great a sensation at his debut he would immediately have blazed into a star of the first magnitude.'' 77

Ellen Tree had the most infectious and memory-haunting laugh on the stage, and many an old-time admirer of the gay and laughing "Beatrice" keeps in the sunniest corner of his heart the echo of the merry peal behind the scenes which announced the approach of Shakspeare's pet hoyden.

Kate Field.

KATE FIELD

WHEN Anthony Trollope wrote of Kate Field, "She is a ray of light to me from which I can always strike a spark by thinking of her," he expressed the feeling that most people had in meeting her, even though it might not have occurred to them to voice the impression. There was in her radiant personality a glow that flashed a lasting light into the lives that came near her own.

While still a school-girl Kate Field had known and loved and been loved by many of the great souls which had been lent to the world for a time to show how grand a thing a human mind could be when God had smiled upon it as it started upon its flight to earth. Among the inspired ones she knew in her early days in Florence were the

Brownings and their circle, who became her life-long friends.

"And you even got something out of the erratic, distorted soul of Walter Savage Landor?" I asked when she talked of those days.

"Oh, that 'Mad Englishman,' as the Florentines called him—I think I did get more of reality and, perhaps, ideality, out of his nature than anybody else ever did; so the people of Florence said. But they did not know him, and never could, though he had lived within view of them a hundred lifetimes. How could the romantic, pleasure-loving Florentines know anything about the storms and dusky calms and deeps and shallows of such a nature as that of Mr. Landor? Mr. and Mrs. Browning were his friends. I think they were born the friends of everybody. Only a few had the advantage of cashing in their cheques on the Browning bank of affection, because ill health kept Mrs. Browning in a secluded life and they were so all in all to each other that they had little need of the outside world. But, oh, how good thoy wore to those who entered their circle! Their friendship radiated blessing upon all who came near. It was natural that they should care for the strange, lonely, burry old man who, having few of his own time to draw into his life circle, went back to the dead ages of Greece and Rome for most of his companions."

"That is what makes it seem so strange that you and Landor should have been such good friends. He was of a long gone yesterday; you are of a to-morrow that we are hoping for— sometime. I cannot see the ground on which you could meet."

"I suppose," said Kate, "that is the very reason that we were interested in each other. He was an antique riddle to me; I must have seemed a crude and bewildering prophecy to him. Whatever may have been the reason, I think the dear old man really was my friend and was glad to see me when I came back to Florence after years of absence. The album of pictures he gave me then, the last time I ever saw him, is one of my treasured possessions now and shall be put into a place that is worthy of it when I am gone.''

The remarkable versatility of Kate Field was indicated by her brilliant conversational talent so well remembered by all who knew her socially, as well as by her success as singer, actress, playwright, lecturer, editor and author, and with it all a faculty which amounted to a positive genius for retaining through life the many friends won by her irresistible charm and kept by her earnest purpose and depth of character.

Kate Field lived a brilliant and fascinating life and had the good fortune, which comes to few toilers, of giving herself to her work up to the last day. 'She spent one morning writing in her vigorous manner upon the subject which had led her upon a tour of investigation in the Hawaiian Islands. At noon she took ship from a neighboring island to Honolulu; the next day, with the Pacific waves all around her as the boat plied its way to port she went to her Eternal Home as calmly as a sunny summer day sinking to rest.

LUCY LARCOM

THROUGH a woodland that was dear to me long ago a streamlet ran, banked with blue and white violets. It rippled down from a mountain and purled through the forest glade over white pebbles that sparkled like jewels through the pellucid water. I had never seen another brook so clear and so limpidly pure. A leaf would now and then drop from a tree bending over, would drift and dance a moment in the air, swerve downward to the water and float like a little boat with a cargo of palpitant hopes bound for a wide unknown sea.

As I watched the ripples and listened to their soft melody there came to my thought some bits of poetry I had seen in a magazine, signed "Lucy Larcom"; an assumed name I had supposed, as it was in the days of alliterative pen-

Lucy Larcom

names. There was the same lilting
music in the lines as in the ripple of the
brook and the purity of thought and
expression were of the same silvery
whiteness. Meeting Miss Larcom I
spoke of what I had though about her
name and she told me that it was from
the old family name "Lark-Holme,"
the home of the larks.

"I do not like it myself as a name to
write under," she said, "for the reason
that it is so likely to be taken for a
cover of a writer's identity."

Lucy Larcom's home was by the sea,
about ten miles from the "Reef of Nor-
man's Woe," but she confided to me
what she regarded as the disloyal fact
that she did not love the sea as much as
the mountains.

"Of course I love the sea," she said.
"I am never tired of the surges that
dash in like race-horses, and reel back
and disappear in the deeps. I like to

see the great waves go by with crests
shining silver in the sun. The grand
anthem that rolls out from the heart of
the ocean fills me with awe. But I do
not need the sea as I need the mountains. They are so strong; they give
protection just by standing like a majestic wall between us and any possible
foe. They are like a great soul reaching
up to the sky.''

Miss Larcom seemed to me the great
soul that aspired aloft, she was so calm
and steady and unmoved by the trivialities that at times sway weaker beings,
and I tried to tell her my thought. She
looked bewildered and said:

''I am only a very small blade of
grass growing at the foot of the
mountain and looking up to my protector.''

The beauty of the sea was enchant-
ment to her and brought to us fairy
glimpses through her poet-eyes:

"High tide, and the year at ebb;
The sea is a dream to-day;
The sky is a gossamer web
Of sapphire, pearl and gray."

In "A New England Girlhood" she
felt, as she expressed it, that she was
"just taking a little journey backward"
into her childhood and the young girlhood spent in the Lowell Mills, where
her first writing was done as a con-
tributor to the "Lowell Offering," from
which a volume of selections was made
and published in London under the title
of "Mind among the Spindles." In a
course of lectures on literature, delivered in Paris, one discourse was devoted
entirely to the significance and merit of
the periodical which was wholly the
product of the Lowell mill-girls.

This was not the least useful period
of Lucy Larcom's education, for in it
she learned many lessons of patience,
industry and aspiration. It cannot be

known how much of her strength of character and wholesome optimism are due to those early years when she studied the harmonies of work and life as she wove her perfect web.

Very Sincerely Yours
Clara Barton

CLARA BARTON

WITH the passing of Clara Barton there went from earth a soul so great that one is awed to helplessness by the effort to measure the height and depth of the Divine Thought that came to humanity in the brave, strong, universal heart of the frail, gentle, soft-voiced "Angel of the Battlefield." She had just returned from a great foreign war when I first drew near enough to her to feel the heartbeat of her sublime love and sympathy.

"How did you first make up your mind to do this great work?" I asked.

"I did not make up my mind," she replied with a smile of wonderment at my question. "Things came to me as if ordered by a world-controlling power. When I was a timid child, afraid of all things, my brother had an illness that

89

was thought to be mortal. In my care for him I lost all thought of self and lived only in my love for him and sympathy with his suffering. For two years my life was wholly absorbed in nursing him and while I was happy and thankful when he came back to life and health, I felt as if my work was over.''

''It was not to be over until you had fulfilled your mission.''

''I never had a mission and don't know what I could have done with one. But I've always had all that I could possibly do and as soon as one thing was done another stepped in.''

''You were one of the first to enlist when the war began, were you not?''

''My enlistment was so unconscious that I had no thought of going out with the army until I was on the field. I was in Washington when the wounded were brought in from Baltimore under the care of Dr. Joseph Stedman, of Jamaica

Plain, whom I saw here in your home
for the first time since that awful day.
I went to the station to meet the soldiers, and their pain and their courage
took possession of me and I felt that
the opportunity to help them was all
that life held for me. When they began
to think again and memories of home
came to them it was a joy unutterable
to write to their loved ones and tell them
that all was well. So the dear ones at
home would send gifts for their boys
and ask me to see that they went to
their destination and in a little while
quantities of things were coming to me
to be distributed where needed. Soon it
became necessary to carry supplies for
the wounded to the front, then came the
battlefield with all its horrors and the
long fight with death, the victory or the
heartbreak at the end. In it all I
learned that life is the giving of oneself
to save others.''

"You are so brave that you can face any danger unafraid."

"I brave? It always seems strange when anyone calls me that. I am the most timid person on earth, I think. I was always afraid of everything except when so absorbed in helping the unfortunate that thought of self was impossible. I never could assert myself in any way except when some one was to be rescued from danger or pain. Even now I would rather work on the field with bullets flying around me, or stand by the guns in battle, than preside at a public meeting."

Clara Barton was a Christmas gift to the world and was most richly endowed with the spirit of that holy day on which she came to humanity. Many women win admiration and fame in the exercise of various gifts but none other has come so near the great pulsing heart of life as she who brought help and comfort not on the battlefield alone but wherever sorrow and calamity had brought desolation.

From her woodland home in Glen Echo her soul passed beyond to the kindred spirits who through sorrow and crucifixion had found Eternal Life. Over almost impassable roads loving friends took her back to her childhood home. In one part of the route it was necessary to go by wagon through ice and snow and the progress was very slow. One of the sorrowful group urged the driver to make all speed he could to catch a boat. He promised to use his best effort, and asked who was in the coffin. Upon being informed he said, "Clara Barton! She saved my father's life when he was wounded in battle. Do not be afraid; do not be afraid; I will take you there in time." So, on her last journey the Angel of Pain was helped along the way by a grateful heart.

MRS. ROBERT EDWARD LEE

WHEN Colonel Robert E. Lee of the United States Army decided to cast in his lot with his native State his wife said to him, "Whichever way you go will be the path of duty. You will think it right, and I shall be satisfied." She bravely kept her word, though years later she could not repress the plaint, "If I could forget my old home I think I should be happy." To forget the beauties and the historic riches of Arlington with its treasure of Washington relics which had come down to the mistress of that magnificent home from her great-grandmother, Martha Custis Washington, was an impossibility. Her thoughts often turned back to the stately mansion and the majestic trees and the clear sweep of greensward stretching down to the river, as she sat in her

Richmond home in a room looking out upon a veranda shaded by ailanthus trees, and knitted socks and gloves for the soldiers, which was all that she could do to help for she could not leave her chair except when she was carried. She and her daughters in one month gave 196 pairs of socks and gloves to one brigade, though she was an invalid and her daughters worked in the city hospitals.

"I am thankful there is one thing I can do," she said putting a newly finished pair of socks on the pile which represented the day's work.

"Who else can do it so well and so quickly?"

"No one else has so much experience. Other people can do other and more important things."

"None of us can do anything as important as you do in setting us an example of patience and calmness. But

95

are you not in your heart wild with joy when General Lee wins?"

"I am thankful, my dear. I know the General always does his best and am content to be quiet when he wins and calm when he loses."

Mrs. Lee took up a pair of socks and began to mend them with fingers so trained to work that they never waited upon conversation.

"I mend the General's socks and give them to the hospital. The head nurse told me that when a man is supposed to be lingering too long in hospital, instead of sending him away they give him a pair of the General's socks and he straightway betakes himself to the field."

"A proof, perhaps, that the influence of a man's spirit remains in everything he has touched."

"Can you knit?" she asked me.

"Not very much. I tried to round

off a heel once." Lest she should think me wholly devoid of useful accomplishments I added, "I can paint."

She laughed.

"I fear that would not be of much use. I think you can sing, too. General Pickett brought another dear little girl to see me once. She was beautiful and was very fond of General Pickett. Now don't be jealous; she was his sister Jinnie. She sang delightfully. Most people open their mouths wide when they sing, but she didn't. She sang every note through a kiss that made it sound like a birdnote."

Sincerity was the leading characteristic of Mrs. Lee. When a friend submitted to her the manuscript of a biography of the General she paused at an anecdote and asked:

"Does that sound like General Lee?"

"Perhaps not," was the reply, "but

it will spoil the whole chapter if I leave out that part.''

''But you don't want to put in anything about General Lee that is not true.''

The anecdote was omitted.

Only once after the heartbreaking parting at the beginning of the war did she see that dear home for which she so longed. All the joys that had once made it an enchanted garden of dreams had changed to ghosts that haunted the sad old place and wailed dirges where in early days she and her boy lover, Robert Lee, had planted an avenue of trees that shaded their walks in after years. She could not endure the loneliness and said, ''Let me get a drink of water from the spring and then take me away.'' She spent some days in Alexandria and on Sunday the young men carried her chair into Christ Church that she might join in the service where her great grandmother had worshipped and where George Washington was a vestryman. In all the Lexington years she was a prisoner to pain and General Lee would always bring in at the eventide the most beautiful event of the day to lighten her clouded life. "Mrs. Lee," he said once, "I have such a nice thing to tell you to-day. I have had a letter from one of 'my boys' and he tells me that he is going to be married and that he wishes me to give his wife the most beautiful bridal present that a woman could desire. He wants me to write her a letter and sign it with my name."

LOUISE CHANDLER MOULTON

IN Number 28, Rutland Square, Boston, there was for many years the best American version of a genuine salon that has ever been known. Not only were the greatest writers of our own country to be found there, but through the graphic delineations given by the hostess, Mrs. Moulton, the best authors of other countries were mentally present. All poet souls recognized her as kindred with themselves and established a bond of sympathy which by radiation extended itself to all who were so happy as to come within her sphere. Mrs. Moulton's mind was a translucent window through which the sun of genius lit the souls of her neighbors. No less was it a creative force to evolve centers of light all its own.

One of the most prized among Mrs. Moulton's friends was the blind poet,

LOUISE CHANDLER MOULTON

Philip Bourke Marston, whose physical eyes had been closed to earthly things that his soul might behold in all their splendor the beauties of earth and sky glorified to the spiritual sight. One of his characteristics was the power to visualize the scenes which were his by internal perception, as when he wrote of the "most exquisite and natural blending of strong emotion with the sense of external nature" in Mrs. Moulton's poetry.

"He seemed to have a supernaturally clear vision," said Mrs. Moulton. "All the great canvas of Nature was spread out to his view and irradiated by his spiritualized imagination."

"His sea poetry is majestic," I said.

"The sadness of the deep voice of the sea appealed to the sorrow in his heart and awakened an echo that brought all the full, deep meaning to the reader."

"The closing of his eyes to the sunlight must have darkened his life in many ways."

"That was his first grief, coming upon him from an accidental blow in play when he was three years old," replied Mrs. Moulton.

"He was blind so young?"

"When some one asked him that question years later he said, 'No, I was not blind then. I could not read, nor see the face of a friend, but I could see the waving of the trees in the wind, catch the glint of gold in the sun, the green of the grass, the glory of sunset and the surging of the waves. It was so different from the black pall that closed around me later.' His mother was his good angel, being eyes and all things for him, sharing his aspirations and seeing his visions. She died when he was twenty. Then his sister Ciceley was everything to him that the devoted

102

mother had been until one sad morning
she died in my room where she was
making me a morning visit. Her father
and brother were absent for a short trip
on the continent. No one else could
ever have been to him what she was,
except her whom he called 'the one
whose love was the chief joy of my life,'
in the pathetic dedication of his first
book of poems, 'Song-tide,' to the
memory of the loving and loyal girl
who would have been his wife had not
death claimed her for a bride. Three
years later his soul-brother, Oliver
Madox Brown, the brilliant boy in the
twentieth year of his poet-artist life,
passed away, and father and son were
left alone with each other and memories. Yet Philip Marston could not be
alone, for he had always his visions,
and I think that never in the world
had any man such friends,—friends
who were lovers, adorers and guardian

angels, attracted to him by his irresistible beauty of face and manner and held enchained by the yet greater loveliness of his soul.''

Though Mrs. Moulton had many friends in her own country, she won her highest appreciation in England. Uncle Sam was still in the struggle for life and prosperity and had not leisure for the delicate aroma of sentiment which gave her melodious lines an irresistible attraction in a circle permeated by the literary spirit of that High Priest of Sentiment, Alfred Tennyson. Her English friends were always held by her in especially loving remembrance.

LOUISA MAY ALCOTT

IN 1869 "Little Women" came into the world and took by storm all young people and all people who had once been young.

Miss Alcott had been known as a writer of fairy tales, had published a volume of "Flower Fables" and had contributed a number of stories to Boston journals. In 1863 she published her experiences in a war hospital, under the title of "Hospital Sketches," having been compelled by the failure of her health to give up the work into which she had put her strength and patriotic enthusiasm. To comfort herself for the disappointment she recorded her war memories, putting into the volume so much of the earnestness and sympathy that had formerly gone into her hospital work that her story reached the hearts of the readers and became a popular book. Some years later her novel of "Moods" was published.

It was not until "Little Women" had been added to the ever-increasing list of Miss Alcott's works that her public became acquainted with the home life and inner thought of the author. It was soon discovered that the "Little Women" were the author and her sisters in the old home at Concord and the interest was as great as that of watching a group of young lives expanding before the eyes of the readers. There was a heart knowledge and a heart interest in the book not to be found in fiction.

Miss Alcott's friends were not only surprised but incredulous when it was discovered that she was the author of the volume in "No Name Series," called "A Modern Mephistopheles." I could scarcely accept the statement when first presented, but it recalled to

106

me a conversation I once had with her in Boston. Speaking of "Little Women" I said:

"The story is so natural and lifelike that it ohowo your truo otylo of writ ing,—the pure and gentle type, with innocent young lives and the events that would inevitably befall bright girls and boys with the thoughts and feelings befitting a quiet loving home circle."

"Not exactly that," she replied. "I think my natural ambition is for the lurid style. I indulge in gorgeous fancies and wish that I dared inscribe them upon my pages and set them before the public."

"Why not?" I asked. "There seems to be no reason why you should not be gorgeous if you like."

"How should I dare to interfere with the proper grayness of old Concord? The dear old town has never known a startling hue since the redcoats were there. Far be it from me to inject an inharmonious color into the neutral tint. And my favorite characters! Suppose they went to cavorting at their own sweet will, to the infinite horror of dear Mr. Emerson, who never imagined a Concord person as walking off a plumb line stretched between two pearly clouds in the empyrean. To have had Mr. Emerson for an intellectual god all one's life is to be invested with a chain armor of propriety.''

''The privilege of having such a Titan of intellect to worship is worth being subjected to some trammels of propriety.''

''And what would my own good father think of me,'' she asked, ''if I set folks to doing the things that I have a longing to see my people do? No, my dear, I shall always be a wretched victim to the respectable traditions of Concord.''

The "No Name" gave poor Louisa an opportunity to escape for a moment from the Concord traditions, and I think she enjoyed the writing of every sentence in the "Mephistopheles."

Perhaps the Seer of Concord never had a more devout worshipper than Louisa Alcott who, when a child, wrote him adoring letters which were never sent. When she was a mature woman with her well-earned honors thick upon her a great sorrow, the death of her best loved sister, May, the "Amy" of "Little Women," was announced first to Mr. Emerson that he might break the tidings gently to her and comfort her with his tender, loving sympathy.

As the home circle narrowed by the passing of its members the tender bond of affection between Louisa Alcott and her father drew yet closer and the feeling of interdependence grew still deeper till death came and the old house was left desolate. At the funeral of Mr. Alcott the mourners were yet more deeply saddened by the message that Louisa had just passed from earth.

CELIA THAXTER

THERE are people who are born for the sea. Life without its white foam-horses galloping shoreward in an endless succession of charges upon the sands and wild dashes backward in ever recurring defeat would be like a symphony without its theme. The melody would fall on silence without the deep basso-profundo of the rolling surges to sustain its rich chords.

Of these was Celia Thaxter. I never think of her without seeing her on Appledore, "Among the Isles of Shoals," with her chains of sea-shells encircling neck and wrists, melting into the soft grayness of her dress that she wore with a simplicity and dignity which made me think her born of the deep gray stately ocean that she loved. Her window gave us a view of the dashing

111

white foam, the middle distant waves,
calm and slow in the majestic silence of
illimitable power, and the far-off per-
spective of high lights and dim shadows
with the sapphirine sky bending to
touch the fading sea-line.

"My love for it has failed but once,"
she said. "Then I was lonely and
wretched for days. There had been a
terrible storm and a ship had gone to
wreck before my eyes. I had seen the
poor creature struggling in the boiling
waves until it parted and the surges
swept over it. No boat could live on
that tempestuous water. The lifeboats
of the ship set out and went down almost as soon as they touched the waves.
Nothing could go out from shore and
the only thing for us was to watch the
storm and its victims to the end."

"It is our helplessness in the storms
of life that breaks our hearts," I
said.

"Most of all I felt the truth of that the next morning. When I saw the poor, pallid, sea-drenched forms upon the beach I raged against the wicked sea for its cruelty. Then reason came and told me that it was not the sea that was cruel; the winds had made a victim of the ocean as well as of the people who had put their trust in boat and wave. The sea was not treacherous; it received them with joy and promised them fair because it wished them well. It would reunite long-parted friends; it would take men and women to new homes to find the peace that was denied them in the land of their birth; it would bear invalids to healthful climes where life and strength and happiness would return. All these things the good, generous loving sea would do, but the cruel winds come and its hopes are lost. For days afterward the surges moaned a dirge for the peaceful dead and the sorrowful living. Since then I have not misjudged my sea and I love it."

"Consider the sea's listless chime:
Time's self it is, made audible,—
The murmur of the earth's own shell."

I quoted.

"You love Rossetti? He hears and sees so many things. Those lines come back to me when I hold a seashell to my ear. It is like the voice of earth. Rushing, moaning, sorrowful, but with a thread of song that is like the faint heralding of a great joy coming in the distance, dimly heard when the soul is a-tiptoe with prophecy, the good time coming when all the earth shall join in the chorus of good will and serene content."

Celia Thaxter's garden was a glory of color and bloom and, walking through its paths, she looked like the goddess of the lilies, regal and fair and sweet. The birds she loved and petted perched on the boughs above and sang for her their most beautiful and happy songs.

"Floworo will livo alwayo for us," she said. "Life could not be without them. I am sure that Keats breathed the fragrance of the narcissus that I saw dying on his grave."

Among her flowers the Angel of the Better Life found her, and loving hands heaped the fragrant blossoms high upon her grave and I think, like Keats, she knew that they were there, and was glad.

MRS. CLEMENT C. CLAY

"THE BELLE OF THE FIFTIES"

THE passing of Mrs. Virginia
Clay-Clopton but a few weeks
prior to the time at which I write
broke a golden link that bound to the
commonplace business era of the present the olden days that have passed
into tradition and romance.

In the golden Fifties when Washington, all unconsciously, was dancing
over a volcano rumbling with the coming eruption the gayest and brightest
and wittiest woman in the brilliant
throng was the beautiful young wife of
Senator Clement C. Clay, who had
come from her secluded Alabama home,
a novice in the social world, timid, as
she has told us, in the presence of an
older belle whom she greatly admired,
and had soon become the radiant center
of the social whirl. Whether she

"With love of Virginia Clay-Clopton
Hunts Ala. May 4th 1912.
"Just as I am"
V. C. C.

sparkled in her natural form as the reigning queen of grace and beauty or appeared in the homely and grotesque guise of Mrs. Partington, convulsing the entire company with laughter, she was supreme. "Clay, you deprived the stage of its most brilliant ornament when you married Mrs. Clay," said a brother Senator to Senator Clay at the Gwyn ball where the pseudo Mrs. Partington filled the ball-room with merriment for the entire evening.

Sometimes such gayety and radiance belong only to the sunshine and when heavy clouds darken the day the evanescent gleam vanishes. The brilliance of Mrs. Clay was a torch illuminating the darkest night. In the Confederacy when gloom and uncertainty hung over all southern hearts her gayety glowed through the darkness and helped her people to endure loss and sorrow.

117

As a hostess Mrs. Clay was superb. Her unlimited hospitality and genius for entertaining overcame the contracted limitations of southern resources in war time and made her home as popular a social center as it had been in the brighter days of her queenship in Washington. Her dwelling was a kind of Liberty Hall in which every comfort that could be obtained was furnished for her guests, and they were permitted to enjoy life as they chose. "Lassie," she said to me once when I had accepted her invitation to spend with her a vacation from school, "I am going to give you a lesson in true hospitality. I shall let you alone. When you want me you will always know where to find me and I shall be glad to have you." I followed her method and had a delightful vacation.

After our marriage the General and I were in Richmond and staying at the

home of Colonel Shields next door to
Mrs. Clay, when the General suggested
one evening that we call on our charming neighbor. While we were there
Senator Vest came in. He was then in
the Confederate Senate; afterward for
many years he served Missouri in the
United States Senate. He had his vio-
lin, which he played very beautifully,
and Mrs. Clay waltzed with the General
as merrily and gracefully as she could
ever have danced at an Embassy ball in
the National Capital when life for her
was one long and brilliant Mayday fes-
tival.

The earnestness and determination
of Mrs. Clay's character were forcibly
shown by her rescue of her husband
from death in his prison cell in Fort
Monroe after the close of the war. Innocent of the charges brought against
him, he voluntarily surrendered himself as soon as he learned of the order

119

for his apprehension. Denied trial, he was held until the rapid failure of his health threatened early death. Mrs. Clay went to Washington to plead with President Johnson for her husband's life. After repeated unavailing efforts to see the President and weeks of anxious waiting she was admitted. It required many interviews to awaken the President to a sense of the injustice of leaving an innocent man to die in a prison cell but after a time, moved by the dominant character and enthusiastic devotion of the wife, he became interested and promised to give favorable attention to the plea. While under the influence of the petitioner's earnestness his promises were very fair, but the vacillating President, after an interview with some opposing politician, would forget his good intentions and lapse into lukewarmness, meeting his importunate visitor upon her next appearance with the assertion of his inability to do anything for her. At last she saw him by appointment in his office one evening and, after pleading her cause anew, told him that she would not leave until she had the order for Senator Clay's release. In vain he sparred for time, asking her to come the next day, promising to sign the order and give it to her when she returned. She had lost faith in promises and positively refused to go without the all important document. In despair President Johnson signed the order and Mrs. Clay before leaving the office sent a telegram of good cheer to the heartsick prisoner.

Mrs. Clay took the Senator to his Alabama home, where she nursed him with a devotion that was never surpassed, but freedom had come too late. A few years later he passed into the eternal freedom of the soul.

In Washington the most intimate friends of Senator and Mrs. Clay were Senator Clopton and his charming wife, who lived next door to the Clays. They all followed the fortunes of the South and some time later Mrs. Clopton died.

Many years after Mr. Clay's death Mr. Clopton one morning called his children into the library and told them that he wanted to consult them about something he wished to do, saying that he would not do it if they objected. When he explained that his desire was to marry Mrs. Clay the unanimous expression of delight assured him of entire acquiescence in his aspiration. One of the most beautiful things in the lovely woman's life was the devotion of her stepchildren.

After Mr. Clopton's death Mrs. Clay-Clopton passed many years of widowhood in which her spirit of laughter never failed her, and her youthful buoyancy remained as of old. Eighty-two years of mingled sunshine and shadow did not prevent her from leading the dance at a Confederate ball given a few years ago, with a step almost as light as that of the Belle of the Fifties or of the matron of the war-crimsoned Sixties.

MARGARET E. SANGSTER

MRS. SANGSTER had been invited down for the week-end to the beautiful home of Mr. and Mrs. William Haxtun, where 1 was a guest on Staten Island, next door to the Appleton house.

One evening when talking of many things old and new, especially old, Mr. John M. Daniel, the great War Editor of the South, came up for discussion and, from her own experience in editorial work, she was much interested in the fierce old editorial fighter.

"I know and love Virginia and Virginians," she said, "and had friends in both armies," and we drifted into stories of war and camp and then into tales of the Old Dominion in war time and before, of the negroes of plantation days, of the Folk Lore of the South and romances of the olden times. Our

Margaret E Sangster.

host, a man of wide business experience and intellectual ability, said:

"As I have listened to you I felt as I did when a boy reading Hans Andersen tales. If I had known what an interesting and fascinating life we were breaking up down there I might have been an anti-Abolitionist."

Very thoughtfully Mrs. Sangster raised her far-seeing eyes that looked only upon good things from the zenith to the dimmest horizon line of her sky and her poetic spirit lighted her gentle face as she said:

"You have had a wonderfully rich life and you are yet but a child. You have had the black mammy and the little colored playmates, the old atmosphere of the romantic South and the plantation life that is all over now. You have had the romance of war, the excitement of the battlefield, the love of the soldiers, the nursing of the

wounded in hospital. You have known
a new country, a new President and
Cabinet and all the great changes of
South and North alike. You have been
the wife of a hero, the mother of children, the mother of an angel and now
the greatest of all sorrows has come to
chasten you, widowhood, and last, the
highest boon that could come with all
these things, the necessity for work. It
is only through pain and loss that we
can gain the joy of effort and the triumph of winning.''

''I have had all and lost all,'' I said.

''You cannot lose what you have had;
it is yours always and the joy of reliv-
ing it in memory and expression will
be the greatest happiness of your life.
Pass it on to the world before you forget, and let the people see the old life
as it was. The soil will not bring forth
anything unless it is cultivated and, as
in the parable, thorns and thistles will

spring up and destroy the good seed. Cultivate the rich ground which will bring you a golden harvest and which can never be known again because its time is over. There can never again be a Confederate President and Cabinet.''

Myra, a little niece of Mr. Haxtun, asked Mrs. Sangster what rebels were. There wasn't anything in the Commandments about them, was there, and did the Bible say what would become of them? She replied:

"My dear, in your history you are taught to respect rebels, though I do not think the Bible or the Commandments say anything about them. You know the Continental Army were rebels and Washington was the greatest rebel of them all. I think they were the only American rebels. Our own Government was founded on the consent of the States with certain conditions provided and when there was reason to withdraw that consent the effort to do so was not rebellion.''

I afterward met Mrs. Sangster at the University of Virginia and we went together to Monticello, the home of Thomas Jefferson. The old homestead was not then, as it is now, beautifully kept as a casket for Jeffersonian relics and memories and the road from the University of Virginia to the mansion of the Father of American Democracy was ''a hard road to travel.'' When we had successfully made the journey Mrs. Sangster said:

''It is almost a pity that the great old Democrat was not born in Boston. Then Massachusetts might have bought the old place and made it a museum filled with the things that were dear to Jefferson, objects that he had touched and loved, a shrine to the memory of the staunch old patriot where his countrymen could meet and renew their own patriotism in the memory of his devotion to his country. Men high in judicial realms, poets and historians, great scientists whose efforts are given for their country's honor, all would have met in the old mansion to seek inspiration from the sacred recollections of the past. A wide and beautiful road would have led from the University which the great patriot founded to the magnificent home in which he dwelt and it would have been known to all the world as the People's Highway."

EMILY VIRGINIA MASON

IN her cosy little Georgetown cottage Miss Emily Mason spent the latest years of her long life and there I visited her often, finding her as strong and agile after having passed the octogenarian line as she had been long years before when we knew each other in old Virginia.

A portrait of her brother, Stevens Mason, hung upon the wall, and I noted its resemblance to pictures of Colonel George Mason of Gunston Hall, the great old patriot and founder of the family in Virginia.

"My brother Stevens was the first Governor of Michigan; he was appointed by President Jackson acting Governor when twenty years old, the only one under legal age who was ever head of a territorial government. When Michigan became a State he was elected

Governor. I made him a long visit there and so for a time was a Wolverine."

"You have been many things in your life, my dear Miss Emily, and still you always remain the same."

"My most exciting visit to the North was made in the beginning of the war when I was called to New Jersey by the illness of my niece who was the wife of an officer on the staff of General Scott. The newspapers promptly heralded me as a spy, paying me the high compliment of regarding me as brilliant enough to take in the plan of a fortification at a glance and subtle enough to act as the arch-conspirator in complicated and daring schemes. They asserted that I was sent by General Beauregard to arouse the Catholics and by Mr. James M. Mason to stir up the Democrats. The only association I found with humanity outside of our own household was in attending early mass, whereupon I was accused of going early to church to confer with my co-conspirators. Existence was lively there but dangerous, and any attempt to escape would have led to my arrest. Some Sisters who thought that I would succeed in getting away sometime brought letters written by wives and mothers to their husbands and sons in Richmond prisons. I dared not try to take them but learned them by heart and afterward had the good fortune to keep my promise to give the messages to the prisoners. Through the kindness of a friendly northern officer I went to Richmond and found myself in about as bad a position as I had held in the North, for I was taken for a spy sent by the Government at Washington. On the way I found my work while waiting on a steamer on which we had taken refuge after an accident

to our own boat. A number of wounded
men were put aboard. I spent the rest
of the waiting time in attending the un-
fortunates and left them in good care
when I went on my way."

"Oh, how well I know what you were
to the hospital service in Richmond, my
dear!"

"Thank you; I did try to do what I
could, and for all alike. It made no
difference whether a wounded man was
northern or southern, if he suffered
and needed care. Our men had the same
spirit and when we divided supplies
with the captives in the city prisons
would send them the white bread, saying that northern soldiers were not
used to corn bread and could not eat
it."

We had never heard of the Red Cross
in those days, but Miss Mason's hospital was managed on the same prin-
ciples. It made no difference what

cause a man supported, the fact that he was suffering brought to him warm sympathy and swift aid.

"I've just had such a sweet visit with Winnie Davis. We talked of you and she said beautiful things about you."

"Yes; we are good friends. When I was in Paris a few years after the war closed Mr. Davis wrote me that Winnie was there in school and asked me to call on her. She was overjoyed to see some one from home who knew and loved her people, and asked many questions about the war. 'But what happened just after the war?' she asked. 'What did Papa do first? I was too little then to know anything about it and no one has ever told me what happened next after the war closed.' I saw that she had been intentionally kept in ignorance and did not tell her, but wrote to Mr. Davis asking him why she had not been told the truth. He replied that he did

134

not wish his daughter to know anything that had happened to him after the fall of the Confederacy because this was her country and he wanted her to live in it and love it, and she never could if she knew what he had suffered."

When I went to see Miss Mason on her ninetieth birthday I found her lying on the sofa, explaining the unusual attitude by saying that she was not feeling quite so well as usual. She spoke of a magazine article which she had written some years before and said that she would go upstairs and get it, as her maid did not know where it was. I begged her not to make the effort, but she said that she was in the habit of walking upstairs and was not so ill as to be unable to go. So she went and soon came down, apparently on the feet of sixteen, which I thought doing well for one of her "ill days." But she always was the youngest woman I knew, whatever she might say of her years. On her ninety-first birthday she received her friends, giving them the welcome of one in the full tide of health and vigor, and enjoying every moment of the day. A short time later she passed from earth.

MRS. ROGER A. PRYOR

WHEN my Soldier was in command of the Department of Virginia and North Carolina and our home was in Petersburg I knew and loved the beautiful and brilliant Mrs. Pryor, so well known for years in old Washington. The deep interest with which I listened to her stories of life in the Capital incited her to tell me many memories of what was to her the brightest time she had ever known, furnishing a wide contrast to those dark days of war and privation. She told me that she had known the "Little Giant" of Illinois and my cousin, Mr. Beverly Tucker of Virginia, who were good friends.

"It was an impressive lesson in contrast to see them together, Judge Douglas, the shortest man in Washington, and Mr. Tucker, almost a giant in

137

height and with weight in proportion.
The Judge really had the fixed idea
that he would be President some day
and had already considered the rewards
which he would bestow upon his friends.
Passing the White House with his tall
friend, Mr. Tucker, he asked with a majestic wave of his hand toward the home
of Presidents, 'Bev, what do you want
me to give you when I go there to live?'
'Not a thing, Douglath,' replied Mr.
Tucker with his fascinating little lisp,
'not a thing. Jutht take me on your
knee and call me Bev.; thath all.' "

Mrs. Pryor laughed anew at the mental picture of that giant Virginian on
the knee of the little Illinoisian.

"When Patti made her debut in 'Lucia' Mr. Douglas listened for a while in
a dazed way and then asked me, 'What
is it all about?' I told him that it was
Scott's 'Bride of Lammermoor' set to
music. He brightened visibly and

138

asked with lively interest, 'Whose bride was she? Where did she live?' I told him I was afraid that she was only a fiction and that she never lived anywhere. 'Then I don't see what she is for,' he replied in a tone of disappointment, and turned away indifferently. His interest lay in acquiring exact information and if 'Lucia' was not an existent fact of life he did not want to hear about her even through the medium of the most glorious voice on earth.''

Mrs. Pryor's experience and the breadth of her observation seemed very wonderful to me and I said, ''I wonder if I shall ever go to Washington and see great politicians and diplomats?''

''If you do, child, it will all be different,'' she said sadly. ''The old life will not come back and the old friends are gone. You cannot see Washington Irving with his scholarly atmosphere and

139

the melancholy romance that always circled him like the fragrance of lavender in an old casket.''

''Why are people who write funny things always sad?''

''Maybe for the reason that we do not see the humor of life until most other things are lost. My friend, Mr. James, is gone, always insistent upon all the alphabet that belonged to him, to the confusion of butlers, who could get innumerable variations from the combination 'G. P. R.' His solitary horseman has ceased to emerge from the wood on successive pages till the reader began to have serious intentions of shooting him from behind a neighboring clump of bushes. How delightful G. P. R. would have been if he had only lived, and not written books. I suppose the man must be better than his book or the book would not be worth much, but I used to think it was not necessary

140

that the discrepancy should be so great."

Mrs. Pryor adorned Washington society at a time when our national history was drifting into its most tragically dramatic stage, but not yet released from the primitive era which regarded the White House as a structure of classic magnificence, and contemplated with admiration tinged with awe Old Hickory in Lafayette Park heroically bestriding his impossible steed and charging rampant over the artistic sensibilities of a helpless populace. The riotous specimens of art hung upon the walls of public buildings had not yet produced in the art-soul a glimmering of cubist nightmares rendered maddening by heterogeneous collections of shingles falling down undiscoverable staircases.

It was an era of political and social brilliance, when eloquent men still thun-

dered forth heroic sentiments in classic
periods, and lovely women had the slop-
ing shoulders and oval faces which have
since given place to the square build
and commercial profile of a business
ago.

With a party of friends Mrs. Pryor
watched the wind-blown snow falling
upon the procession that escorted the
youthful and handsome President
Pierce to the White House and to his
political death. She was a distin-
guished social figure in the administra-
tion of President Buchanan, which went
its dancing, laughing, sparkling way to
meet the earthquake. She was a noble
woman of the Confederacy and lived
many years after its fall to give to the
reading world beautiful pictures of the
lights and shadows that had fallen over
her life.

SARAH ORNE JEWETT

MISS JEWETT was the faithful delineator of the life and character of old New England, as is Mary Wilkins Freeman of the New England of to-day. The daughter of the village doctor, the little Sarah Orne unconsciously absorbed the life of her environment as she drove with her father when he made his professional calls.

"The best of my education was received in my father's buggy and the places to which it carried me," she said. "The rest was mere schooling. With the wicked connivance of my father I used to run away from school and go the rounds with him; if we suffered a little from the pangs of our New England conscience we enjoyed enough from the delightful experience to make up for it.

In the spring days the new opening beauties of the countryside fascinated me as I sat in my father's buggy and waited for him to finish his visit and go on to the next patient. The loveliness of sky and trees and flowers and soft carpet of grasses filled my soul with happiness. What dreams used to come to me up that long brown road leading off to fairy places in some entrancing Nowhere. When the professional call was long and the visions faded away I would go into the yard and play with the children who always brought me something new in childish character and point of view. When people sometimes remark upon the realistic personality of one of my book children I go back in thought to some moment of childish play and say, 'That did not take any work. It is just a child I knew once, lifted out of those days and feloniously transferred to my book. I ought to be

144

arrested for kidnapping, because it was nothing else.' "

"If more people could kidnap to such good effect that crime would become the crowning virtue of the age," I replied.

"It would be a crime or a virtue easily achieved if the world had the advantages that were thrust upon me without my seeking. A dull little country village is just the place to find the real drama of life. In the roar of the city it is only the glaring virtues and the strident vices that become apparent. The delicate cadences are lost in the blare of the heavy tones."

"You learned to hear more of the cadences and see more of the shades of character than most people do."

"The village doctor comes nearer than anyone else to the true springs of village life, nearer even than the pastor of the one little church that points to the only way to heaven for all alike.

The preacher, however great-hearted, comes with the mystifications of the spirit life that people like to hear about on Sunday mornings when they don their Sunday clothes and come together for their weekly sermon and chat in the churchyard after service is over. But the Doctor brings comfort and healing for the earth life, which they think they understand because there is no one to tell them there is anything to it except what they can see. I, being his other self, came next in intimacy, and the characters I met when the Doctor made his rounds became a part of my very life."

"I always wondered why your people seemed like old friends to me."

"They were actual discoveries. In one house lived 'Aunt Tempy' and watching the quiet way in which she passed on the small blessings of life, the kindly smile, the gentle word, the helping hand, the gift from her own small store to some one who had even less, I was unconsciously evolving the 'Aunt Tempy' whose passing would leave so wide and deep a void. In another poor little home was the self-abnegating milliner, longing for a wider opportunity to make some one else happy, and in a more imposing dwelling the rich lady of the little community, who would have enjoyed being liberal, had not some dead hand of her ancestors stretched out through the generations and held her back from the indulgence of generous impulses. So there were 'Aunt Tempy and her Watchers' ready to hand.''

"I know the glory of that kind of life. My first memories, even before I was able to ride alone, are of sitting in front of my father on horseback and riding through the countryside. And now work is all the more enjoyable, begun in such a beautiful way."

"I love the thought part of it and the weaving part, but the business phase is not so agreeable. I wonder if in the next life our thoughts will not grow like the wild flowers in the woodland and blossom and breathe fragrance and glow with color and light all unconnected with the book market."

In this era of futurist nightmares and cubist spasms the clear etchings traced by Sarah Orne Jewett are crowded out of the gallery of time, but we who knew her as a living presence like to go back and revel in the silvery light of her exquisitely drawn and delicately shaded word pictures of the quiet scenes in which she found the dramatic forces of life cast in the comedy and tragedy of everyday existence.